The Way of the Cross for the Holy Souls in Purgatory

REVISED

Susan Tassone

Our Sunday Visitor Publishing Division
Our Sunday Visitor, Inc.
Huntington, Indiana 46750

Nihil Obstat: Rev. Michael Heintz
Censor Librorum

Imprimatur: ✠ John M. D'Arcy
Bishop of Fort Wayne-South Bend
November 18, 2004

The *nihil obstat* and *imprimatur* are declarations that a work is free from doctrinal or moral error. It is not implied that those who have granted the *nihil obstat* and *imprimatur* agree with the contents, opinions, or statements expressed.

The Stations of the *Way of the Cross for the Holy Souls in Purgatory* appearing in this book were originally published by: *Frank Quin & Company,* Philadelphia, copyright © 1928.

The Scripture citations used in this work are taken from the *Catholic Edition of the Revised Standard Version of the Bible* (RSV), copyright © 1965 and 1966 by the Division of Christian Education of the National Council of the Churches of Christ in the United States of America. Used by permission. All rights reserved.

Our Sunday Visitor Publishing Division
Our Sunday Visitor, Inc.
200 Noll Plaza
Huntington, IN 46750

ISBN: 1-59276-141-0 (Inventory No. T192)

LCCN: 2004114346

Cover design by Monica Haneline
Interior design by Sherri L. Hoffman

Mosaics in this book have been provided courtesy of the Marytown/Shrine of St. Maximilian Kolbe, 1600 W. Park Avenue, Libertyville, IL 60048. The photo of the House of Ephesus on page 8 has been provided courtesy of Mary's Media Foundation, Rye, New York. The image of Our Lady of Ephesus, by Bob Smith, on page 10 has been provided courtesy of the Basilica of the National Shrine of the Immaculate Conception. The photo on page 64 has been provided courtesy of the author (© *L'Osservatore Romano,* Vatican City).

PRINTED IN HONG KONG

Who is without an interest in purgatory? Who has not, somewhere, a treasure buried in that dreary casket called a grave? And had they none, were they of the few who have never lost a friend, should their interest in purgatory be any less strong and deep, since God's friends are there and God desires them elsewhere?

Reflect on what you do when you aid to release one of these prisoners of love.

You free a soul from dire woe, from inexpressible suffering; you add a citizen to heaven; you give joy to the angels and saints; you comfort and delight Jesus and his Mother Mary.

SISTER CHARLES BORROMEO, O.S.D.

Contents

Origin of the Way of the Cross

*W*ho was the first to meditate on Jesus' bitter passion? Who was the first to return to the path of Calvary? Who relived the unspeakable pain and sorrow of Our Savior's death? His suffering Mother. Our Mother.

How did the devotion of praying the Way of the Cross begin?

There is a pious tradition that the Way of the Cross originated with the Blessed Virgin Mary, who visited these places after Our Lord's ascension. She confirmed her commitment to devotional prayers in a vision to St. Brigid. In the revelations to Blessed Anne Catherine Emmerich, Our Lady continued her meditations of the Way of the Cross that she herself erected behind her home in Ephesus, in what is now western Turkey.

Devotion to the Passion of Christ became widespread in the twelfth and thirteenth centuries. Upon their return home, Crusaders constructed stone tablets depicting various places they had visited in the Holy Land. This devotion, known as the Little Jerusalem, demonstrated how widespread the custom of praying at the Stations had become. In their cemetery in

Antwerp, Franciscan friars set up Stations representing the Seven Sorrows of the Blessed Virgin Mary.

In 1342, when the Franciscans took over the custodial care of the holy places in Palestine, part of their mission was to promote devotion to the Passion of Christ. The Stations of the Cross became popularized in monasteries, chapels, and throughout the world. For many centuries, the Way of the Cross was done in reverse order, starting at Mount Calvary, with pilgrims tracing their steps back to Pilate's Palace or the Garden of Gethsemane. The number of Stations, or "stops," varied, with as many as thirty at one time. Pope Clement XII fixed the number at fourteen in 1731.

St. Leonard of Port Maurice, an advocate for the holy souls, promoted this devotion with such enthusiasm that he became known as the Preacher of the Way of the Cross. He said, "If you deliver one soul from purgatory, you can say with confidence, 'Heaven is mine.'"

The House of Ephesus

But standing by the cross of Jesus were his mother and his mother's sister, Mary the wife of Clopas, and Mary Magdalene. When Jesus saw his mother, and the disciple whom he loved standing near, he said to his mother, "Woman, behold your son!" Then he said to the disciple, "Behold your mother!" And from that hour the disciple took her to his own home. (John19:25-26)

St. John brought the Blessed Mother to Ephesus after the death of Jesus. Here Our Lady would spend the last nine years of her earthly life. Her home was rediscovered in 1891 through the study of the revelations of Blessed Anne Catherine Emmerich (1774-1824), stigmatist, visionary, and prophet, who was born in Westphalia, Germany. In her book, *The Life of the Blessed Virgin Mary*, Anne describes Mary's "Holy Way of the Cross":

> Behind the house, at a little distance up the hill, the Blessed Virgin had made a kind of Way of the Cross. When she was living in Jerusalem, she never failed, ever since Our Lord's death, to follow his path to Calvary with tears of compassion. She had paced out and measured all the distances

between the Stations of that *Via Crucis*, and her love for her Son made her unable to live without this constant contemplation of his sufferings. Soon after her arrival at her new home, I saw her every day climbing part of the way up the hill behind her house to carry out this devotion. At first she went by herself, measuring the number of steps, so often counted by her, which separated the places of Our Lord's different sufferings. At each of these places she put up a stone, or if there was already a tree there, she made a mark upon it. The way led into a wood, and upon a hill in this wood she had marked the place of Calvary, and

MARY'S HOUSE IN EPHESUS

the grave of Christ in a little cave in another hill. After she had marked this Way of the Cross with twelve Stations, she went there with her maidservant in quiet meditation: at each Station, they sat down and renewed the mystery of its significance in their hearts, praising the Lord for his love with tears of compassion. Afterward she arranged the Stations better, and I saw her inscribing on the stones the meaning of each Station, the number of paces and so forth. I saw, too, that she had cleaned out the cave of the Holy Sepulchre and made it a place for prayer. At that time, I saw no picture and no fixed cross to designate the Stations, nothing but plain memorial stones with inscriptions; but afterward, as the result of constant visits and attention, I saw the place becoming increasingly beautiful and easy of approach. After the Blessed Virgin's death, I saw this Way of the Cross being visited by Christians, who threw themselves down and kissed the ground.

In 1961, Blessed Pope John XXIII reconfirmed the plenary indulgence for pilgrims visiting the House of Ephesus. In 1967, Pope Paul VI visited this important Marian shrine, as did Pope John Paul II in 1979 when he celebrated Mass there. Millions of tourists of every faith visit Mary's house in Ephesus year-round, and many miraculous cures and favors have been granted to pilgrims.

These fourteen Stations to Freedom are lovingly dedicated to Our Lady of Ephesus

The Importance of the Way of the Cross

The Way of the Cross represents the sorrowful journey that Jesus made with the cross to die on Calvary. The Church teaches that the souls in purgatory undergo a process of purification that must include suffering. By praying and making sacrifices for the holy souls, you have the power and privilege to relieve their pain. If your heart is inclined to bleed for them, as does the Sacred Heart of Jesus, please pray this Way of the Cross. In return, their gratitude will bring you countless blessings. May a stream of mercy flow from you to the holy souls in purgatory.

An Act of Contrition

O my Jesus! I love you above all things. I hate and detest all my sins, because by them I have offended you. The holy indulgences, the fruits and merits of this devotion, I intend to gain for the souls in purgatory, in particular for those who in life were near and dear to me, and also for those for whom I am, in a special way, obligated to pray.

O Mary, my merciful Mother and the Mother of the poor souls in purgatory, accompany me, by your intercession, on this journey.

The First Station

Jesus Is Condemned to Death

V. We adore you, O Christ, and we praise you.

R. Because by your holy cross, you have redeemed the world.

O my innocent Jesus, to free me from eternal death, you allowed yourself to be condemned by a pagan judge to the death of the cross. Give me a hatred for sin and the grace to so live that I may one day obtain from you a merciful sentence.

The poor souls in purgatory have already been judged. Through your mercy, they have escaped hell; yet on account of their sins, your justice has caused them to suffer the pains of purgatory.

O most merciful Jesus, have pity on them. Revoke the sentence of their exile and open to them the gates of heaven.

My Jesus, mercy!
Our Father... Hail Mary...

V. Eternal rest grant unto them, O Lord.

R. And let perpetual light shine upon them.

Merciful Jesus, grant them eternal rest. Amen.

The Second Station

Jesus Is Made to Bear His Cross

V. We adore you, O Christ, and we praise you.

R. Because by your holy cross, you have redeemed the world.

O holy cross, you are the tree of life, the gate of heaven, our salvation, and our only hope. Be my salvation at the hour of death.

O Jesus, be mindful of your servants who have departed this life with this sign of faith. Free them by the victorious power of your cross, by which you have conquered death. Lead them into eternal life and happiness.

My Jesus, mercy!
Our Father... Hail Mary...

V. Eternal rest grant unto them, O Lord.

R. And let perpetual light shine upon them.

Merciful Jesus, grant them eternal rest. Amen.

The Third Station

Jesus Falls the First Time

V. We adore you, O Christ, and we praise you.

R. Because by your holy cross, you have redeemed the world.

O Jesus, through your weakness under the cross and the merits of this first fall, grant me perseverance in keeping my good resolutions, that I may always walk faithfully in your holy ways. The souls in purgatory now suffer because they neglected and abused your graces in this life. They now realize that no sin-stained soul can see God. Therefore, have mercy on them, and cleanse them from all sin.

Through the intercession of your sorrowful Mother, deliver them from purgatory.

My Jesus, mercy!
Our Father... Hail Mary...

V. Eternal rest grant unto them, O Lord.

R. And let perpetual light shine upon them.

Merciful Jesus, grant them eternal rest. Amen.

The Fourth Station

Jesus Meets His Afflicted Mother

V. We adore you, O Christ, and we praise you.

R. Because by your holy cross, you have redeemed the world.

O Heart of Mary! O Heart of Jesus! I offer my life for my sins. May the sweet names of Jesus and Mary be on my lips and in my heart at the hour of my death. O sweetest Heart of Jesus, I implore that I may love you more and more. Sweet Heart of Mary, be my salvation.

Mother most sorrowful, merciful Queen of the Holy Souls, into your hands I place my few merits and implore you to unite them with the infinite merits of your Son. Offer them to the eternal Father for those souls who are bound to me by ties of relationship.

Mother of Mercy, pray for them.

Mother of Sorrows, console them.

My Jesus, mercy!
Our Father... Hail Mary...

V. Eternal rest grant unto them, O Lord.

R. And let perpetual light shine upon them.

Merciful Jesus, grant them eternal rest. Amen.

The Fifth Station

*Simon of Cyrene Helps Jesus
to Carry His Cross*

V. We adore you, O Christ, and we praise you.

R. Because by your holy cross, you have redeemed the world.

O my Jesus, I accept the cross. I embrace it. Let me help you to carry your cross, by being patient in all trials that may assail me.

How many souls in purgatory now regret their past impatience! But you, O Lord, be generous with them and remit all that still remains to be expiated.

My Jesus, mercy!
Our Father... Hail Mary...

V. Eternal rest grant unto them, O Lord.

R. And let perpetual light shine upon them.

Merciful Jesus, grant them eternal rest. Amen.

The Sixth Station

Veronica Wipes the Face of Jesus

V. We adore you, O Christ, and we praise you.

R. Because by your holy cross, you have redeemed the world.

O Lord, Jesus Christ, you who have left on Veronica's veil the image of your bloodstained countenance, grant that the memory of your bitter passion and death may ever remain impressed on my soul. Have pity on the poor souls, made to your image and likeness and redeemed by your Most Precious Blood. Free them from all sin, that they may enter heaven and see you face-to-face forever.

My Jesus, mercy!
Our Father... Hail Mary...

V. Eternal rest grant unto them, O Lord.

R. And let perpetual light shine upon them.

Merciful Jesus, grant them eternal rest. Amen.

The Seventh Station

Jesus Falls the Second Time

V. We adore you, O Christ, and we praise you.

R. Because by your holy cross, you have redeemed the world.

*M*y sins have made your cross heavy, O Jesus. I detest them and firmly propose to amend my life.

Never permit me to separate myself from you again.

Have mercy, O Jesus, on those souls who now suffer the pains of purgatory for mortal sins committed in this life.

O clement Heart of Jesus, have compassion on them.

My Jesus, mercy!
Our Father... Hail Mary...

V. Eternal rest grant unto them, O Lord.

R. And let perpetual light shine upon them.

Merciful Jesus, grant them eternal rest. Amen.

The Eighth Station

Jesus Comforts the Women of Jerusalem

V. We adore you, O Christ, and we praise you.

R. Because by your holy cross, you have redeemed the world.

*M*ost compassionate Heart of Jesus! My Jesus, who said to the holy women, "Do not weep for me, but weep for yourselves and for your children" (Lk 23:28), make me weep for the ingratitude that I have returned for your love. I wish to make amends in this life for my sins, that I may obtain pardon for them in the next.

Grant me a tender love for the souls in purgatory, especially for the souls of my relatives. For the future, I promise to do what I have neglected through my forgetfulness and hardness of heart.

My Jesus, mercy!
Our Father... Hail Mary...

V. Eternal rest grant unto them, O Lord.

R. And let perpetual light shine upon them.

Merciful Jesus, grant them eternal rest. Amen.

The Ninth Station

Jesus Falls the Third Time

V. We adore you, O Christ, and we praise you.

R. Because by your holy cross, you have redeemed the world.

Through this most painful fall, O Jesus, I ask you to deliver me from an unhappy death, which would plunge me into hell. From the power of the enemy deliver my immortal soul, and make me live and die in your grace.

Look with mercy upon the poor souls doing penance in purgatory. With tears and prayers they seek your help and mercy. Hear their prayers and lead them out of that place of purification into the blessed peace of heaven, there to enjoy forever the splendor of your glory.

My Jesus, mercy!
Our Father... Hail Mary...

V. Eternal rest grant unto them, O Lord.

R. And let perpetual light shine upon them.

Merciful Jesus, grant them eternal rest. Amen.

The Tenth Station

Jesus Is Stripped of His Garments

V. We adore you, O Christ, and we praise you.

R. Because by your holy cross, you have redeemed the world.

*M*y most blessed Redeemer, stripped of your garments for love of me, grant me holy modesty and purity.

Deliver me from all dangerous inclinations to created things. Make me die to everything of this world, that at death separation from all earthly things may be easy. Of what benefit now are wealth and the pleasures of this world to the souls in purgatory? Their bodies they had to leave to decay and the dust of death, and their wealth to heirs. Only their works have followed them: the good to be rewarded, and the evil to be punished.

O Lord, put an end to their suffering. Do not keep them any longer from the inheritance of the saints, but pardon them and admit them into the realm of eternal bliss and happiness.

My Jesus, mercy!
Our Father... Hail Mary...

V. Eternal rest grant unto them, O Lord.

R. And let perpetual light shine upon them.

Merciful Jesus, grant them eternal rest. Amen.

The Eleventh Station

Jesus Is Nailed to the Cross

V. We adore you, O Christ, and we praise you.

R. Because by your holy cross, you have redeemed the world.

*M*y most innocent Jesus, nailed to the cross for my sins, I beseech you through the merits of your horrible suffering to come to my aid in my last sickness and agony. Grant me the grace to receive in time your most holy sacraments. Come to me, then, O Most Holy Viaticum, and pour into my soul the patience of your Most Sacred Heart! And you, O Mary, my Mother, console me in that hour and make sweet my sufferings, through the sorrow that pierced your heart at the Crucifixion.

Lamb of God, have mercy on the souls in purgatory, whose sufferings are greater than those of all the sick and dying. Spare them this agony, and through the merits of your passion admit them into eternal dwellings.

My Jesus, mercy!
Our Father… Hail Mary…

V. Eternal rest grant unto them, O Lord.

R. And let perpetual light shine upon them.

Merciful Jesus, grant them eternal rest. Amen.

The Twelfth Station

Jesus Dies on the Cross

V. We adore you, O Christ, and we praise you.

R. Because by your holy cross, you have redeemed the world.

O Jesus, through your three hours' agony on the cross, grant me a happy death. Take me when I am best prepared. In that hour, fill my soul with holy sentiments of faith, hope, and charity. Grant me true and perfect contrition for my sins and the grace to accept with Christian resignation my death, with all its pains and sufferings.

May I leave this world invoking your Most Holy Name.

Mary, Mother of Sorrows, refuge of the dying, be near me in my last agony.

Remember, O most loving Jesus, the poor souls with that love with which you gave comfort to the good thief: "Today you will be with me in Paradise" (Lk 23:43). Call these souls into the kingdom of your glory, that they may praise you together with all of the angels and saints forever.

My Jesus, mercy!
Our Father… Hail Mary…

V. Eternal rest grant unto them, O Lord.

R. And let perpetual light shine upon them.

Merciful Jesus, grant them eternal rest. Amen.

The Thirteenth Station

Jesus Is Taken Down from the Cross

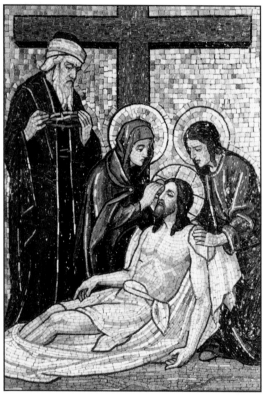

V. We adore you, O Christ, and we praise you.

R. Because by your holy cross, you have redeemed the world.

O Jesus, you whose soul descended to the dead to announce peace to the just of the Old Testament, descend now among the poor souls who yearn for you. Free them from the chains of their slavery, and grant them the liberty of true children of God! O Mary, my Mother, may I, like Jesus, be placed in your arms at my departure from this world. Be with me at the tribunal of the Divine Judge, that through your intercession I may obtain a favorable judgment.

Sweet Heart of Mary, be my salvation!

My Jesus, mercy!
Our Father... Hail Mary...

V. Eternal rest grant unto them, O Lord.

R. And let perpetual light shine upon them.

Merciful Jesus, grant them eternal rest. Amen.

The Fourteenth Station

Jesus Is Laid in the Tomb

V. We adore you, O Christ, and we praise you.

R. Because by your holy cross, you have redeemed the world.

O Jesus, through the merits of your bitter passion and death, and through your glorious resurrection, I beseech you to have compassion on the poor souls, and to grant them a happy and glorious admission into heaven. Let them enter into that peace so long desired. Let them contemplate the splendor of the Beatific Vision. Let them bless eternally your mercy.

Sweet Heart of Mary, be my salvation, that I may not be condemned to that place of agony, when my body will be in the cold earth. Let my soul flee the fires of purgatory. Most loving Mother, on that day save your child. Bring me quick relief, and through your merits deliver me from the flames, that I may thank you in heaven and, with you and all the saints, adore and love Jesus, your beloved Son, who with the Father and the Holy Spirit lives and reigns, true God, forever and ever. Amen.

My Jesus, mercy!
Our Father… Hail Mary…

V. Eternal rest grant unto them, O Lord.

R. And let perpetual light shine upon them.

Merciful Jesus, grant them eternal rest. Amen.

Closing Prayer

O my crucified Redeemer, I offer you this devotion, which, by your grace, I have just finished. Grant that the precious fruits of your death on the cross be not lost either for me or for the souls in purgatory. Mary, Mother of Sorrows, place my petitions in the Heart of your beloved Son, so that I may be admitted into the kingdom of grace, there together with my dear ones, both living and dead, to be blessed eternally.

O Gentlest Heart of Jesus, ever present in the Blessed Sacrament, ever consumed with burning love for the poor captive souls in purgatory, have mercy on them. Be gentle in your judgments, but let some drops of your Precious Blood fall upon the devouring flames. O merciful Savior, send your angels to conduct the poor souls to a place of refreshment, light, and peace. Amen.

V. Eternal rest grant unto them, O Lord.

R. And let perpetual light shine upon them.

V. Sacred Heart of Jesus, have mercy on them.

Merciful Jesus, grant them eternal rest. Amen.

Eucharistic Exposition and Benediction for the Holy Souls in Purgatory

Exposition Hymn: "O Salutaris Hostia" ("O Saving Victim")

All: (Recite Psalm 130 on page 56)

Priest: Let us pray. Have mercy, O gentle Jesus, on the souls detained in purgatory. You who, for their ransom, took upon yourself our human nature and suffered the most cruel death, pity their sighs and the tears shed when they raise their longing eyes toward you. And by virtue of your passion, cancel the penalty due to their sins. May your Blood, O tender Jesus, your Precious Blood, descend into purgatory to give solace and refresh those who languish there in captivity. Reach forth your hand to them, and lead them into the realm of refreshment, light, and peace. Amen.

Reading: Revelation 7:9-17

Homily

Quiet Reflection

Litany of the Most Precious Blood for the Holy Souls

Lord, have mercy on us.   **Lord, have mercy on us.**
Christ, have mercy on us.   **Christ, have mercy on us.**
Lord, have mercy on us.   **Lord, have mercy on us.**
Christ, hear us.   **Christ, hear us.**
     Christ, graciously hear us.

God, the Father of heaven,   **Have mercy on us.**
God, the Son, the Redeemer of the world,
     Have mercy on us.
God, the Holy Spirit,   **Have mercy on us.**

Most Precious Blood of my Redeemer,
     Save them, O Lord.
Blood of the new, eternal Testament...
Price of our redemption...
Fountain of living water...
Precious ransom of sinners...
Pledge of eternal salvation...
Sacrifice to eternal justice...
Key to the gates of heaven...
Purification of our poor souls...
Salvation in our misery...
Remedy for our wounds...
Forgiveness of our sins...
Payment of our debts...
Remission of our punishment...

Source of salvation...
Hope of the poor...
Nourishment of the weak...
Healing balm for the sick...
Reconciliation of sinners...
Joy of the just...
Refuge of all Christians...
Admiration of the angels...
Consolation of the patriarchs...
Expectation of the prophets...
Strength of the apostles...
Confidence of the martyrs...
Justification of confessors...
Sanctification of virgins...
Refreshment of the suffering souls...
Beatitude of all saints...

Be merciful.	**Spare them, O Jesus.**
Be merciful.	**Hear them, O Jesus.**

R. Amen.

The Hail Mary *(adapted for praying for the holy souls in purgatory)*

Priest: Let us commend the holy souls to the intercession of Our Lady, their Mother, by praying her prayer.

(The congregation prays the words of the Hail Mary and then pauses while the priest or reader offers the reflection.)

HAIL MARY… Behold, most merciful Mother, your poor and sorrowful children who suffer so grievously in the purification of purgatory. We beg you, for the sake of the great joy that the angelic salutation caused you, to have compassion on them, and send them your holy angel to bring them another joyful greeting, and to announce to them release from their sufferings.

FULL OF GRACE… Obtain for them grace, mercy, and remission of the great cleansing they now endure.

THE LORD IS WITH THEE… He will deny you nothing, but will hear your prayer and mercifully come to the assistance of these poor souls.

BLESSED ART THOU AMONG WOMEN… Yes, you are blessed among all creatures in the whole world! Bless and render happy with your intercession the poor imprisoned souls, and deliver them from their bonds.

AND BLESSED IS THE FRUIT OF THY WOMB, JESUS… Your Son is the Savior and Redeemer of the whole world, who was born, without pain, of you, a Virgin! O merciful Jesus, blessed fruit of Mary's inviolate virginity, have mercy on the souls departed! O merciful Mother, hasten to their assistance!

HOLY MARY, MOTHER OF GOD… Wonderful Virgin Mother of God!

PRAY FOR US SINNERS… — and for the souls in purgatory.

NOW… — and forever!

AND AT THE HOUR OF OUR DEATH… And as you assisted the departing souls in their last agony, so assist them now in their grievous suffering, that delivered by your motherly intercession they may pass from present suffering to everlasting joy, from anguish and torment to everlasting rest and glory, and rejoice with you and the whole heavenly host through all eternity.

AMEN.

Adoration: "Tantum Ergo" ("Down in Adoration Falling")

The Divine Praises

Blessing and Reposition

Closing Hymn: "Holy God, We Praise Thy Name"

(Other appropriate prayers and songs may be substituted.)

Scripture Reflections

John 6:40

"For this is the will of my Father, that every one who sees the Son and believes in him should have eternal life; and I will raise him up at the last day."

2 Maccabees 12:42, 44-45

They turned to prayer, beseeching that the sin which had been committed might be wholly blotted out.... For if he were not expecting that those who had fallen would rise again, it would have been superfluous and foolish to pray for the dead. But if he was looking to the splendid reward that is laid up for those who fall asleep in godliness, it was a holy and pious thought. Therefore, he made atonement for the dead, that they might be delivered from their sin.

Additional Scripture Passages for Reflection

Psalms 23 and 26; Matthew 5:26; 1 Corinthians 3:15; Revelation 21:27; Zechariah 13:9; Sirach 7:33; Isaiah 25:6-9; Romans 5:5-11 and 8:11; Mark 15:33-39 and 16:1-6; Luke 7:11-17.

Seven Penitential Psalms

*M*any of the psalms are lamentations and calls for help. Since the seventh century A.D., the seven Penitential Psalms have been used by the Church to express repentance for one's personal sins and the social evils of society. These psalms contain sorrowful expressions as well as words of confidence, hope, and thankfulness to God. The sinner entrusts himself to the loving mercy of God.

During his last illness, St. Augustine requested that these psalms be copied out and put on the wall beside his bed. The dying saint read them continually, shedding copious tears.

David wrote many of the one hundred fifty psalms. As you pray these psalms, pray from the heart as David did.

Psalm 6

Prayer in Ordeal

O LORD, rebuke me not in thy anger,
    nor chasten me in thy wrath.
Be gracious to me, O LORD, for I am languishing;
    O LORD, heal me, for my bones are troubled.

My soul also is sorely troubled.
But thou, O LORD — how long?

Turn, O LORD, save my life;
deliver me for the sake of thy steadfast love.
For in death there is no remembrance of thee;
in Sheol who can give thee praise?

I am weary with my moaning;
every night I flood my bed with tears;
I drench my couch with my weeping.
My eye wastes away because of grief,
it grows weak because of all my foes.

Depart from me, all you workers of evil;
for the LORD has heard the sound of my weeping.
The LORD has heard my supplication;
the LORD accepts my prayer.
All my enemies shall be ashamed and sorely troubled;
they shall turn back, and be put to shame in a
moment.

Psalm 32

Prayer of Admission of Sin

Blessed is he whose transgression is forgiven,
whose sin is covered.
Blessed is the man to whom the LORD imputes no
iniquity,

and in whose spirit there is no deceit.
When I declared not my sin, my body wasted away
 through my groaning all day long.
For day and night thy hand was heavy upon me;
 my strength was dried up as by the heat of summer.

I acknowledged my sin to thee,
 and I did not hide my iniquity;
I said, "I will confess my transgressions to the LORD";
 then thou didst forgive the guilt of my sin.

Therefore let every one who is godly offer prayer to thee;
at a time of distress, in the rush of great waters,
 they shall not reach him.
Thou art a hiding place for me,
 thou preservest me from trouble;
 thou dost encompass me with deliverance.

I will instruct you and teach you
 the way you should go;
 I will counsel you with my eye upon you.
Be not like a horse or a mule, without understanding,
 which must be curbed with bit and bridle,
 else it will not keep with you.

Many are the pangs of the wicked;
 but steadfast love surrounds him who trusts in the
   LORD.
Be glad in the LORD, and rejoice, O righteous,
 and shout for joy, all you upright in heart!

Psalm 38

Prayer in Distress

O LORD, rebuke me not in thy anger,
    nor chasten me in thy wrath!
For thy arrows have sunk into me,
    and thy hand has come down on me.

There is no soundness in my flesh because of thy
    indignation;
there is no health in my bones because of my sin.
For my iniquities have gone over my head;
    they weigh like a burden too heavy for me.

My wounds grow foul and fester because of my
    foolishness,
I am utterly bowed down and prostrate;
    all the day I go about mourning.
For my loins are filled with burning,
    and there is no soundness in my flesh.
I am utterly spent and crushed;
    I groan because of the tumult of my heart.

LORD, all my longing is known to thee,
    my sighing is not hidden from thee.
My heart throbs, my strength fails me;
    and the light of my eyes — it also has gone from
        me.

My friends and companions stand aloof from my
    plague,
  and my kinsmen stand afar off.
Those who seek my life lay their snares,
    those who seek my hurt speak of ruin,
    and meditate treachery all the day long.

But I am like a deaf man, I do not hear,
    like a dumb man who does not open his mouth.
Yea, I am like a man who does not hear,
    and in whose mouth are no rebukes.

But for thee, O Lord, do I wait;
    it is thou, O Lord my God, who wilt answer.
For I pray, "Only let them not rejoice over me,
    who boast against me when my foot slips!"

For I am ready to fall,
    and my pain is ever with me.
I confess my iniquity,
    I am sorry for my sin.
Those who are my foes without cause are mighty,
    and many are those who hate me wrongfully.
Those who render me evil for good
    are my adversaries because I follow after good.

Do not forsake me, O Lord!
    O my God, be not far from me!
Make haste to help me,
    O Lord, my salvation!

Psalm 51

Prayer for Remission of Sins (also known by its Latin title, Miserere, *"Have mercy")*

Have mercy on me, O God,
    according to thy steadfast love;
    according to thy abundant mercy blot out my
        transgressions.
Wash me thoroughly from my iniquity,
    and cleanse me from my sin!

For I know my transgressions,
    and my sin is ever before me.
Against thee, thee only, have I sinned,
    and done that which is evil in thy sight,
so that thou art justified in thy sentence
    and blameless in thy judgment.
Behold, I was brought forth in iniquity,
    and in sin did my mother conceive me.

Behold, thou desirest truth in the inward being;
    therefore teach me wisdom in my secret heart.
Purge me with hyssop, and I shall be clean;
    wash me, and I shall be whiter than snow.
Fill me with joy and gladness;
    let the bones which thou hast broken rejoice.
Hide thy face from my sins,
    and blot out all my iniquities.

Create in me a clean heart, O God,
  and put a new and right spirit within me.
Cast me not away from thy presence,
  and take not thy holy Spirit from me.
Restore to me the joy of thy salvation,
  and uphold me with a willing spirit.

Then I will teach transgressors thy ways,
  and sinners will return to thee.
Deliver me from bloodguiltiness, O God,
  thou God of my salvation,
  and my tongue will sing aloud of thy deliverance.

O LORD, open thou my lips,
  and my mouth shall show forth thy praise.
For thou hast no delight in sacrifice;
  were I to give a burnt offering, thou wouldst not be
    pleased.
The sacrifice acceptable to God is a broken spirit;
  a broken and contrite heart, O God, thou wilt not
    despise.

Do good to Zion in thy good pleasure;
  rebuild the walls of Jerusalem,
then wilt thou delight in right sacrifices,
  in burnt offerings and whole burnt offerings;
  then bulls will be offered on thy altar.

Psalm 102

Prayer in Misfortune

Hear my prayer, O LORD;
  let my cry come to thee!
Do not hide thy face from me
  in the day of my distress!
Incline thy ear to me;
  answer me speedily in the day when I call!

For my days pass away like smoke,
  and my bones burn like a furnace.
My heart is smitten like grass, and withered;
  I forget to eat my bread.
Because of my loud groaning
  my bones cleave to my flesh.
I am like a vulture of the wilderness,
  like an owl of the waste places;
I lie awake,
  I am like a lonely bird on the housetop.
All the day my enemies taunt me,
  those who deride me use my name for a curse.
For I eat ashes like bread,
  and mingle tears with my drink,
because of thy indignation and anger;
  for thou hast taken me up and thrown me away.
My days are like an evening shadow;
  I wither away like grass.

But thou, O LORD, art enthroned forever;
    thy name endures to all generations.
Thou wilt arise and have pity on Zion;
    it is time to favor her;
    the appointed time has come.
For thy servants hold her stones dear,
    and have pity on her dust.
The nations will fear the name of the LORD,
    and all the kings of the earth thy glory.
For the LORD will build up Zion,
    he will appear in his glory;
he will regard the prayer of the destitute,
    and will not despise their supplication.

Let this be recorded for a generation to come,
    so that a people yet unborn may praise the LORD:
that he looked down from his holy height,
    from heaven the LORD looked at the earth,
to hear the groans of the prisoners,
    to set free those who were doomed to die;
that men may declare in Zion the name of the LORD,
    and in Jerusalem his praise,
when peoples gather together,
    and kingdoms, to worship the LORD.

He has broken my strength in midcourse;
    he has shortened my days.
"O my God," I say, "take me not hence
    in the midst of my days,
thou whose years endure
    throughout all generations!"

Of old thou didst lay the foundation of the earth,
    and the heavens are the work of thy hands.
They will perish, but thou dost endure;
    they will all wear out like a garment.
Thou changest them like raiment, and they pass away;
    but thou art the same, and thy years have no end.
The children of thy servants shall dwell secure;
    their posterity shall be established before thee.

Psalm 130

Prayer Imploring God's Mercy (also known by its Latin title, De Profundis, "Out of the depths")

Out of the depths I cry to thee, O LORD!
    LORD, hear my voice!
Let thy ears be attentive
    to the voice of my supplications!

If thou, O LORD, shouldst mark iniquities,
    LORD, who could stand?
But there is forgiveness with thee,
    that thou mayest be feared.

I wait for the LORD, my soul waits,
    and in his word I hope;
my soul waits for the LORD
    more than watchmen for the morning,
    more than watchmen for the morning.

O Israel, hope in the LORD!
    For with the LORD there is steadfast love,
    and with him is plenteous redemption.
And he will redeem Israel
    from all his iniquities.

Psalm 143

Prayer of Humble Entreaty

Hear my prayer, O LORD; give ear to my supplications!
    In thy faithfulness answer me, in thy righteousness!
Enter not into judgment with thy servant;
    for no man living is righteous before thee.

For the enemy has pursued me;
    he has crushed my life to the ground;
    he has made me sit in darkness like those long dead.
Therefore my spirit faints within me;
    my heart within me is appalled.

I remember the days of old,
    I meditate on all that thou hast done;
    I muse on what thy hands have wrought.
I stretch out my hands to thee;
    my soul thirsts for thee like a parched land.

Make haste to answer me, O LORD!
    My spirit fails!
Hide not thy face from me,

lest I be like those who go down to the Pit.
Let me hear in the morning of thy steadfast love,
    for in thee I put my trust.
Teach me the way I should go,
    for to thee I lift up my soul.

Deliver me, O LORD, from my enemies!
    I have fled to thee for refuge!
Teach me to do thy will,
    for thou art my God!
Let thy good spirit lead me
    on a level path!
For thy name's sake, O LORD, preserve my life!
    In thy righteousness bring me out of trouble!
And in thy steadfast love cut off my enemies,
    and destroy all my adversaries,
        for I am thy servant.

Reflections of the Saintly Ones

St. Thomas More

[Speaking for the holy souls in *The Supplication of Souls*] Friends and every good Christian man and woman: Open your hearts and have pity upon us. If you believe not that we need your help, alas, what lack of faith! If you believe our need and care not for us, alas, what lack of pity. For whoever pity not us, who can you pity? If you pity the blind, there is none so blind as we which are here in the dark till some comfort come. If you pity the crippled, there is none so crippled as we, that can neither put one foot out of the fire or have one hand at liberty to defend our face from the flame. If you have been sick and longed for day, while every hour seemed longer than five, think what a long night we souls endure that lie sleepless, restless, burning and broiling in the dark fire one long night of many days, of many weeks, and some of many years.

St. Catherine of Genoa

Souls in purgatory unite great joy with great suffering. One does not diminish the other. No peace is comparable to that of the souls in purgatory, except that of the saints in heaven. On the other hand, the souls in purgatory endure torments which no tongue can describe and no intelligence comprehend, without special revelation. (Treatise on Purgatory)

St. Pio of Pietrelcina

The holy souls are eager for the prayers of the faithful which can gain indulgences for them. Their intercession is powerful. Pray unceasingly. We must empty purgatory!

St. Maria Faustina Kowalska

I saw my guardian angel, who ordered me to follow him. In a moment, I was in a misty place full of fire in which there was a great crowd of suffering souls. They were praying fervently, but to no avail, for themselves; only we can come to their aid.... Since that time, I am in closer communion with the suffering souls. (Diary 20)

St. Bridget

[A voice from the depths of purgatory] May those be blessed, may those be rewarded who relieve us in these pains! ... O Lord God, show thy almighty power in rewarding a hundredfold those who assist us by their suffrages, and make the rays of the divine light to shine upon us.

[The voice of an angel] Blessed be upon earth those who, by their prayers and good works, come to the assistance of the poor suffering souls.

Venerable Mary D'Antigna

Know, my daughter, that the Stations of the Cross are most profitable to the holy souls, and constitute a suffrage of the greatest value.

St. Gertrude the Great

Eternal Father, I offer thee the Most Precious Blood of thy divine Son, Jesus, in union with the Masses said throughout the world today, for all the holy souls in purgatory, for sinners everywhere, for sinners in the universal Church, those in my own home and within my family. Amen.

St. Leonard of Port Maurice

If a ray of heavenly light could draw aside the veil from your eyes, you would see these suffering souls hovering around each Station, with upraised arms imploring you, "Have pity on me, have pity on me! In pity for us, make the Way of the Cross for me, your father, your mother, your friend."

Blessed Pope John XXIII

The memory of those who have gone before us, to whom we are linked by bonds of fidelity and gratitude, must also accompany us in all the acts of our daily life. For this is the memorial that they deserve; this redounds to their honor; this is the spirit of Christian prayer for the dead, which is inseparable from Christian life and practice.

Gaining Indulgences With the Stations of the Cross

This plenary indulgence is granted the Christian faithful who devoutly make the Stations of the Cross. It is required only that one devoutly meditate upon the passion and death of the Lord.

This devout exercise must be performed before the Stations of the Cross that have been properly erected.

Movement from one Station to the next is required. If this devout exercise is carried out publicly and such movement by all present cannot be done without some disorder, it is sufficient that the person who is leading the exercise move from Station to Station while the others remain in their places.

People who are legitimately prevented from fulfilling the above requirements can obtain this indulgence if they at least spend some time — for example, fifteen minutes — in devout reading and meditation upon the passion and death of Our Lord Jesus Christ. (Adapted from *The Handbook of Indulgences*, 1986)

Conditions for Receiving This Plenary Indulgence

- Reception of sacramental confession.
- Reception of Holy Communion.

- Performance of the Stations of the Cross.
- Prayer for the Pope's intentions — for example, the Our Father, the Hail Mary, or any pious prayer.
- All conditions must be met within eight days prior to or after the work.
- The person must be in the state of grace and have no attachment to any sin, including venial sin. Otherwise, venial sin renders only a partial indulgence.

The hearing and speech impaired can gain these indulgences by praying the Stations mentally. The person doing the work may personally gain the benefit of the indulgence or apply it to a particular deceased soul. It can be applied generally to the holy souls in purgatory in the manner known to God alone. A plenary indulgence may be gained only once a day, with the exception of the Apostolic Blessing for those on the verge of death. A partial indulgence may be gained as many times as the Stations are prayed. The fruitfulness of the indulgence depends on the spiritual disposition with which the work is performed.

A Word About Gregorian Masses

Gregorian Masses are thirty Masses offered consecutively for one deceased soul. For more information, write to Susan Tassone, c/o Our Sunday Visitor, 200 Noll Plaza, Huntington, IN 46750. (You are encouraged to put these Masses in your will.)

About the Author

Susan Tassone is the author of *Praying in the Presence of Our Lord for the Holy Souls*, *The Rosary for the Holy Souls in Purgatory*, *Thirty-Day Devotions for the Holy Souls*, and the CD *Prayers of Intercession for the Holy Souls* (with Father Benedict Groeschel, C.F.R., and Father John P. Grigus, O.F.M. Conv.), all published by Our Sunday Visitor. *The Way of the Cross for the Holy Souls in Purgatory* has sold more than 50,000 copies. Susan holds a master's degree in religious education from Loyola University of Chicago and is the founder of the Holy Souls Mass Apostolate.

POPE JOHN PAUL II RECEIVES *THE WAY OF THE CROSS FOR THE HOLY SOULS IN PURGATORY* FROM SUSAN TASSONE. THE HOLY FATHER GAVE THE WORK HIS APOSTOLIC BLESSING.